Morocco
Atlas and Sahara
Stephen and Scharlie Platt

www.leveretpublishing.com

Morocco Atlas and Sahara
First published - May 2017
Published by
Leveret Publishing
56 Covent Garden, Cambridge, CB1 2HR, UK

ISBN 978-0-9957680-4-8

© Stephen Platt 2017

All rights reserved. No part of this publication may be reproduced, stored in a retrieval system or transmitted in any form by any means, electronic, mechanical, photocopying, recording or otherwise, except brief extracts for the purpose of review, without the written permission of the publisher.

Morocco
Atlas and Sahara

Morocco 2017

Fez

Sunday 2 April
We are in our new home in the Medina in Fez – sounds of children playing outside, flapping wings of pigeons on the roof terrace. Malachi wants to sleep up here. I don't imagine he will stick to it. I made tea, and Fran and I chatted

while Scharlie slept a little.

    It is a lovely house on five floors with steep tiled challenging stairs. It's clean and quiet and Moroccan, and the plumbing works! The owner, "Sheffield Steve", is from Chesterfield and he spent eight months renovating it. It's in the very heart of ancient Fez. Steve spent a while settling us in and Marc manages to get the telly going just in time to see Cambridge lose the boat race again, although it was very close.

It was hot when we arrived at the airport and Steve had sent a driver to meet us. The highway into town was lined with olive groves and families picnicking in the shade, a Sunday afternoon occupation. It was a half an hour's drive to the western end of the Medina, called the Batha Square after the nearby hotel. From there we walked a twisty route to our house just off the main thoroughfare, the Tala Sghira, that was lined with shops selling fabrics, pottery, leather and metal work, and other tempting goods. It's friendly and not at all threatening, only the children are impish.

After a rest and the boat race we went out to eat at a restaurant called the Ruined Garden. From the main street, we wandered down a narrow alley – faded glory of carved balconies and decorated doorways. The restaurant must be popular because most of the tables were reserved. But they found a nice place for us and we ordered – a choice of soups to start, – chickpea and tomato or broad bean and garlic. Then main courses of meatballs in tomato with egg, or chicken with lentils and vermicelli that looked like cabbage. We played cards and had bread and olive oil, mint tea and olives while we waited for our meal. The waiters were polite and attentive.

Now it is 8:30 PM and we have returned from supper and getting ready

for bed, tired after an early start this morning. Excited happy shrieks rise from children playing in the alley in the cool of the evening, the Iman's call to prayer.

Monday, 3 April
We slept well. Sheffield Steve came at 9 to take us to breakfast at his hotel. His two guides are busy today so we said we find our own way around. This small hotel is nice. It's old and renovated in a similar style to our house. The breakfast spread was delightful – cereal, coffee and three kinds of bread. The cook was a tubby middle-aged lady. She seemed severe but then she offered to refill our coffee cups with a big smile.

We set to explore the two main shopping streets. We found the Madrasa Bou Inania and paid 20 Dirham (dh) each to go in. Despite the many tourists it was tranquil and pleasant. Fabulous limestone carved walls and woodwork;

Madrasa Bou Inania

lots of women posing for photographs. In general, there are fewer tourists than usual the traders say but a sudden influx of Asians fill the courtyard and the guides happy.

We wandered on towards the square where we arrived yesterday. Mouthwatering food stalls of fruit and vegetables and spices. We bought olives

and bread, which tastes much fresher and less salty than in the UK, avocados, peppers and cucumber. The meat being chopped from whole animals looks good, but we are squeamish and avert our gaze. Carts pulled by mules and donkeys share the thoroughfare with pedestrians. We have seen no dogs but there are cats everywhere. People treat them kindly and put out food, but many are very thin.

We went into a telephone shop and bought cheap phones to keep in touch. On the way back to our house Steve bought slippers he saw in a shop front. So he's done all his shopping. Scharlie hasn't started yet, having so far only managed to buy postcards.

After lunch Scharlie, Fran and Malachi went shopping. They returned about five. Malachi had bought a woollen jacket with a hood. He has a clear idea of what he likes and wants a school satchel made from leather and carpet. Scharlie is attracted by so many things, especially the Berber carpets which are quite different from anything she's seen before. Fran is pretty good at saying, "not now", which takes the pressure off.

Fran had a brief rest and then she, Marc and Steve set off again to walk up to the Batha Square where we caught a taxi to the new town to hire a car. We found the Avis office and were shown a car that would do, a Peugeot 308. We

went back to the office to do the paperwork, but it was too expensive nearly twice what we had expected from the Internet. So we decided to check out Hertz and Budget. We passed a local hire car firm and went in. They said they had a car but wouldn't tell us the price. The said to wait five minutes or so and someone would come. But Fran got frustrated and Marc didn't like them not giving a price, so we left. There was a brisk lady in the Hertz office who offered us a similar car to the Avis at the same price. But she also told us that it would be cheaper booking online, so we decide to do it later.

We caught a taxi to the main supermarket we'd seen on our way here. We bought snacks and stuff for lunch while travelling and water.

While we were out trying to hire a car, Malachi watched TV and Scharlie sat on the rooftop in the cool of the evening. "The shadows are getting longer and the birds finding roosting places with much chirping. But the dome of the sky is still powder blue and southeast over the sandy coloured rooftops it looks as if you could run and leap across the entire city. The buildings are tight together and fit in any which way they can as they prop each other up, with steep staircases and jumbled flat roofs and awnings and skylights punctured by the spikes of minarets. There is the smell of baking bread and the faint thud of a football and children's voices for below. It is so calm. A pale vanilla

coloured cat is confidently pacing the rooftop parapets attracted by the birds. The way people live here soothes nerves jangled by the speed of technology and rushing about. A collared dove lands on the TV aerial above with its pink feet, rosy in the sunlight."

That evening we went to Chez Rashid, a restaurant that had been recommended by Steve. It is on the main street and you can watch the world go by while you eat. The food was good and the service fast and pleasant.

Tuesday, 4 April
We slept well last night in smooth ironed white sheets and didn't hear the call to prayer.

This morning our street was almost empty with just a few shops opening their shutters and the smell of tantalising fresh doughnuts. We have breakfast at Steve's main house, beautifully prepared with blue-and -white crockery and silver, strawberries, apples, bananas, sliced and arranged in a circular pattern, a corn bread pancake with butter, marmalade and honey, orange juice just squeezed, cereal, coffee and tea.

We lingered over the meal and chatted to Steve who told us he bought the house eight years ago. It needed a lot of work. He's done it well. He said that most of the tiling, which we had admired, and the plastering, was new. They had kept as much as they could of the old tiles and made new panels on the floor and then offered them up and poured liquid cement in behind them. The carving and metalwork is also very fine.

He had hoped to find us a guide to introduce us to the city. But all the ones he trusted are booked, so instead he marked places of interest on our map. Fran and Steve have a pretty good sense of direction so we should be okay. Sheffield Steve says the house is full, so he's been camping in the office for two weeks and living out of a suitcase.

He bought the house were staying in because a cousin said she wanted to buy and then pulled out. We joked about the stairs. He said there was nothing he could do to make them easier. They are particularly difficult – large tiled uneven spaced rises. France said that the metal stairs to the roof terrace were particularly difficult. He laughed and said they had done them while he was away and when he came back and discovered how uneven they were it was too late. Fran said she had the same problem commissioning work in Morocco. It was part of the charm of the place.

We went back to the house and managed to book a car online with Hertz. Finally we set off down the hill and headed for the East End of town and the Al Quaraouiyine Mosque. The way narrows on Tala' A Kbira, the other main street, parallel to our own. This is at the first confusing since the map shows it widening. It's because they have fitted in an extra street of shops. We went into the Madrasa next to the mosque. But when I went to enter the Mosque itself the guardian on the door asked if I was Muslim. I said, no. He said it was forbidden to non-Muslims and patted me on the shoulder in a friendly way. So

we went into simple cafe next door and had coffee and almond juice.

We came to a junction and were photographing an ornate door in the mosque when a friendly man with a moustache accosted Fran in English and asked if she would like to buy the door and he could get it shipped over. Like

London Bridge, said Fran. They got chatting. We asked him about the palace behind him. He said it was a carpet Institute supported by the government. Over 1,000 women exhibited their carpets here. He made it sound like a museum. I asked if we could come in. He was very welcoming and it dawned

on me that they were selling carpets. Scharlie described what she was looking for and his two helpers began to pull out Berber carpets. He said that they were embroidered by two women who pass the needle from one side to the other, saying "Choo" which means, "look out". So the Berber women making these carpets are called Choo-Choo.

The Berber carpets were particularly fine. Scharlie fell in love with one of them and we narrowed our choice down. The colours could not be more perfect for Leveret Croft, she said. Fran said, you couldn't put that in the kitchen! It can be scrubbed, he said.

We sat chatting convivially about how they were made and finally Steve asked could we get onto price. The man consulted the label sewn on the back of the carpet and then his calculator and said 22,000dh. I translated this as £200 until France said £2,000. He checked his calculator again and said £1,800. He said he could pack it small. I said, we hadn't intended to spend so much. He gave us his card and we said we'd check the size with our son Jon and comeback and negotiate.

We went on a short while and came to another square of metalworkers. We could hear them first – a cacophony of banging on metal, with deep and high-pitched sounds overlapping. Scharlie stopped to look for a metal tray but

didn't buy one. From here we head downhill, slowly, because we are continually accosted by shopkeepers and hangers-on who want to guide us. We got to the tannery and a shopkeeper showed us where we could climb up onto the terraces and get a bird's eye view of the tannery. He gave us sprigs of mint. For the smell, he said.

A young man explained the process. There are vats of salt and pigeon poo to begin cleaning the hides, and then the dye vats for colour. They're doing browns this week so the colours are more muted than the reds and yellows blues and greens of some weeks. We look down on a pallet of many round pools each filled with brown liquid. The colours are all from natural sources like bougainvillea. A dark skinned man with very long legs is stomping up and down in one of the vats, immersed up to his middle thighs.

We sent spent some time in a leather shop attached to the tannery. Fran wanted to buy some goat hides. Goat hides are smaller and finer than cow skins. I watched a man scrape hides with a curved blade, cutting them to achieve the desired thickness. A skilled job, but tiring. There was a large pile of shavings. In the event Fran didn't buy because she thought they were too expensive and she could get the same for less in England.

Everywhere we go the merchants talk of organic sourced material and

handmade lasting quality. Scharlie is tempted by a deep brown, richly textured leather pouf, which reminds her of childhood and would make extra seating at home.

We walked in a big circle and we find our way back to the mosque. Scharlie acquired a man selling silver bracelets. He was very persistent and got into a row with Fran saying how she was spoiling his sale. I checked Scharlie really wanted to buy. She said she was interested, so I left her to it.

The man asked for 120dh for the bracelet saying they had been made

hand-made. "I come from the mountains. They are Berber and made of silver, see the stamp. My wife made these. You're my first customer." Who knows, did it seem plausible?

Scharlie played hard to get. The man followed us down the alley, a constant patter, the price reducing as we went on. It came down to 50dh. Scharlie said twenty and was obviously walking away. Her liberal instincts pricked, thinking, "he needs to make a living, so why should we make a fuss over a pound or two". He can see the uncertainty and confusion in her eyes. He takes a bangle and scrapes it on the pavement. "See, it's real, it doesn't scratch off." She wants

one, but walks off. He follows. Fran interjects again and he makes a dismissive gesture with his arms and a toss of his head. "I am from the mountains; 20dh is for plastic." "Your mother wants it, don't interfere", he tells Fran.

    We are coming to the end of the alley and will turn off soon. Fran has done the bargaining, all Scharlie needed to do was emote and be unable to make up my mind. She finds her voice and offers 30dh for just one, she says. He disputes bit can hear the finality in her voice. He grabs the bangle and puts it on her wrist, showing her how to open it. She has a 20dh note and Fran has 10dh so he won't have to ask for change. Scharlie exchanges the bangle he has put on her for one with flowers. He gives a broad smile; it's a game. He has made a sale even if his profit is small. We turn up the familiar alley to home. Scharlie was pleased the first time she'd haggled, she said.

We get back home and have a late lunch. After a brief rest we sally forth again. Malachi wants to visit the ruins we can see on the hill from the roof terrace of our house. They are the Merenid Tombs. The cliff caves attracted him, but it looked like a long and dusty walk.

Malachi found the way easily. Cutting through the Medina, now much more confident of direction, we left the old city through a gate in the city wall, straight into modern Morocco with broad asphalted curving highways, villas behind high walls, bright with scarlet and pink bougainvillea.

As we are passing the old city wall Malachi and Fran set off up a dirt path. Scharlie and I follow and scramble up to the walls. We scramble past the shallow caves on a sandy slippery path up a crumbling section of the old wall and skirt round till we can cross the grassy valley to the highway leading to the tombs. It's green at this time of the year and families are picnicking on the grass below us.

We climb to the ruins and get a panoramic view of the old city. The sun is beginning to set allowing us to see the High Atlas, covered in snow, far to

the south. A couple of women and children sit in the shade under a tree, with a donkey resting nearby. We climb the steep grassy slope to the ridge dominated by a monolithic arch and guarded by two equestrian policemen. Maybe they have been muggings here, it seems an obvious place. Bright orange and yellow and purple flowers spread their petals in the bright sun. The view of the whole city is clear and understandable from here. We can work out where

our house is and the Batha gate, and in the far distance black smoke curls up from a ceramics works smudging the clear blue sky.

Rather than walk back down to the city we skirt the hillside, following a line of parks. This is where Moroccan families come at this time of day to perambulate and sit – old ladies muffled up as if it's winter. It proved to be a long way round. But it was interesting seeing local families taking their evening stroll or playing with children. The bright colours of the women in their long tunics with covered heads seem completely in keeping here.

We reached a cemetery we have seen from the hilltop ruins. Fran and Steve go to investigate. A youth sitting on a wall gesture does through. But the graves are tight packed and there was no obvious way through. Steve retreats, but Fran wants to take photographs. Another youth arrives and aggressively blocks her path, talking in slurred French, and asks for money. They had "junkies eyes", she said later. It was true – their eyes had a fuzzy, lost look that made your spine tingle. The boy has a chest-thrusting standoff with Marc before backing off.

We walk down to the main avenue instead, just as dusk was falling. It was the highlight of the walk. High walls were pierced with holes, homes to the many swifts that were whistling over our heads and shooting at high speed

into their black burrows.

We reach a gate into the old town and crossed a huge square where many Moroccan families were seated on tiered steps. They find us interesting, especially Malachi with his long blonde hair. We had hoped to get to the Mellah, the Jewish Quarter, we'd read about.

We walk by the side of the botanical garden, with its tall date palms and canals. It is closed at this time of the day. We pass the palace and were going downhill away from the city. We are tired, our spirits flagging, and we give up at a roundabout and head back into the old town. We found a restaurant, having let ourselves be caught by the first person touting for business, and had the usual mix of tagine, couscous and kebabs. It was after eight o'clock and we had walked a long way. Back to the house and pack ready for the morning.

Desert

Wednesday, 5 April   Fez to Timnay, Midelt

We had breakfast at Steve's place again. We had to go back to our house to collect our bags and then fight our way back up the hill through party after party of guided early morning tourists. Mohammed had organised a driver and we got to the airport to rent a car without incident and sat on a wall in the sun while Fran and Marc got the vehicle. We wondered how we would find our car, but a cheerful man with a clipboard spotted us. With Marc installed at the wheel we set off out of the city.

Olive groves interspersed with half-finished luxury homes, new housing estates and flocks of brown Berber sheep. Marc drove sedately in top gear, which Fran, being a snappier driver, found difficult. We left the outskirts of Fez, finally climbing into the Middle Atlas. All is newly green and the trees are coming into leaf. It was fine in the back of the car with Malachi and Scharlie.

We begin the gentle climb to Ifrane; a place we had been told would be good to stop. It seemed to be the site of one of the royal palaces with

manicured lawns and much too spruced up to capture our interest. But the road ran through a "forest of cedars", a national park. Some of the trees were huge.

The road continued to rise and the countryside became greener with small orchards of exquisitely trained apples and apricots. We are heading for a pass through the mountains and the trees give way to low scrub and alpine plants. In a week or two this will be alive with colour but now it looks much like our English moorland, in hues of brown shading into sandy coloured pointy mountains.

Malachi wanted to know why the road didn't go straight up the mountain if it was supposed to reach the other side. He remarked that "at school we had to draw a mountain, and now here we are among them! It's really beautiful". He is a very good traveller. Taking the middle seat in the back with only an occasional plea to have a turn in the front. We listened to Bob Marley on the music channel which we sing along to.

Past Timahdite, we spot a winding stream in time for a late lunch, with poplar trees where people are picnicking. We park and ford the stream with our bag of food and find a nice spot on the grass next to a cedar tree. We spread out our bread and cheese and salad. Steve makes sandwiches, cutting

the whole baguette lengthways, buttering it and adding jamon serrano, cherry tomatoes and cucumber. A friendly white dog waits patiently for us to finish eating before sniffing around for crumbs. Malachi builds a dam in the turgid water. Mark washes his hands thoroughly when we climb back into the car.

The road twists downwards. We see a sign for the lake we have spotted on the map, Aguelmame de Sidi-Ali, and we turn off on a bumpy dirt road for a mile or so. The crystal blue lake is surrounded by mountains and there are still patches of snow on the north facing slopes. But the lake seems low for this time of the year.

In front of the parking place there is a raised viewing stand surrounded by smashed green glass – Heineken bottles as it turned out. Malachi sets off towards the lake down the large pitted volcanic boulders and we follow. Fran says she feels like swimming. It must be cold in the melt water. She paddles and Malachi slips on a rock as he is trying to balance and soaks himself. He is upset. He can't take off his trousers as he failed to wear underpants this morning, he confesses. Then he realises, that since he is already wet, he can play, and he cheers up. The hot sun soon had him dry.

We hang around for a while enjoying the view. It's austere and beautiful. Scharlie says we are a week early since everywhere is about to burst into

flower. She says there are many species of wild flower in the turf.

We set off again to climb the Col du Zad. Malachi has been tracing our altitude on my watch. We reach 2,700 m and then drop down into the desert plain, the aptly named Plateau de l'Arid. It's a barren land of stony earth and strange tabletop hills. But there are olive groves, fruit trees and flocks of sheep in the places near the river.

We find the Ksar Timnay hotel easily on the road somewhere before Midelt. We go to our rooms. There is a pool – that's why Francis chose it. And she and Malachi go swimming. Scharlie and I change but only Scharlie swims; it's too cold for me. I sit in the sun and read my book and watch the others and two young storks on the chimney opposite. The stalks are standing and clacking their beaks loudly. One of them tests its wings and suddenly takes flight. Its twin looks bereft. But later they were both gone. Smaller birds are making a home in their huge nest of sticks. Dinner is better here than in Fez, but the bed and pillow are too hard for Scharlie. Nevertheless we get a good nights rest.

Thursday, 6 April, Midelt to Merzouga

We get up fairly late and are last at breakfast. Scharlie likes the corn cake and take some for lunch. Malachi goes swimming again.

It's a long journey today, but we leave late about 11:30, with Marc driving again. We climb into the mountains and stop at a supermarket in the Midelt. We also find a small shop selling bread. The sun is hot but the breeze is cooling when we get out of the car.

There is an amazing amount of new building and development. There has been recent extensive landscaping and tree planting. Midelt and the next town, Er Rachidia, both look prosperous – lots of banks hotels and luxury homes.

Outside Er Rachidia there was a long avenue of newly planted date palms, promenade and lines of park benches, but nothing but flat stony desert either side of the road. In places, plots near the road that are clearly earmarked for development, are surrounded by mud block walls. Further out of town the plots are marked by piles of stones or merely by a shallow ditch cut into the sand.

On the map we have seen signs of an oasis, the Source Bleu de Meski. I fancied stopping here for lunch and sure enough we come to a wide river with running water. Up to now all the riverbeds, gullies and gorges have been dry.

We stop where there seems to be away down the steep bank to a stand of cane that offers shade. We climb-down with the lunch bag and make sandwiches while Malachi goes to explore the river. He and I throw stones for a while trying to skim to the opposite bank.

I find a soft spot in the grass and rest my back against the cane. A man comes down from the road. I expect him to say we shouldn't be on his land or ask us for money, but he just smiles and says welcome and gives me a thumbs up. When we return to the car we find he has placed a palm branch on the wind screen to shade it.

We follow a line of oases south along the River Ziz. If we had more time it would be nice to explore the oasis villages but we were tired and want to get to our hotel before it gets dark.

We listen, half dozing, to the Hitchhiker's Guide to the Galaxy on Fran's iPlayer. Then we were flagged down by a policeman. It seems we have been doing 76 in a 60 km zone. The policeman was polite but firm. 66 Ok; 76 a problem, he says. Marc is apologetic. While they were doing the paperwork I watched Moroccan drivers creep past. This straight stretch of road out in nowhere is obviously a money-spinner that is well known to the locals.

Finally we reached Erfud and then Rissani, the gateway to the desert, and left the highway. This flat stony plain is the Tafilalt. I had been expecting a dirt road to Merzouga but it was hardtop, straight and narrow. We could see huge dunes the distance, like a mountain range.

We were tired and frazzled by the time we reached Merzouga and we didn't know where to find the hotel. Fran rang for directions but they were unclear. The man kept saying follow your Google Satnav, which wasn't much help. We kept being accosted by men on motorcycles in blue djellabas with black turbans.

Finally we figured out that we have to retrace our steps. We had driven right to the end of the town where the dunes started because Fran new that the place we were staying in was next to the dunes.

I got the Google map out of the boot and we managed to

find the police station and post office which the man had mentioned and turned off the main road and found the village where our hotel was supposed to be. There was a dusty square and a couple of shops. We were directed around the square and down a side road. It seemed improbable but we found a discreet hand-painted sign that read Hotel and Restaurant Fatima. We found a hippy looking cafe. We couldn't believe it and drove round to the square again. A thin dark face man with a scar on his lip came and told us we were in the right place.

The man could tell Marc and Fran were disappointed. He said, no problem. If we didn't want to stop he wouldn't charge us and will help us find somewhere else. France said it was just that it wasn't what we had expected.

He offered us tea and suggested we rest before he showed us the rooms. Marc asked to see the rooms first. Scharlie liked it. I checked the pool for Malachi. It looked nice. I said let's stay here. Marc came back and said the rooms were fine – whole apartments in fact.

We settle down, drive round with our bags and go back to the hotel for dinner. We should have said we wanted to eat since the food is prepared fresh and takes a while. For speed, Scharlie and I decided on omelette and salad and the others had chicken skewers again. It was good. The man came

to talk to us. I asked his name – Hamid. I introduced us. He said he was married to a Japanese lady. Scharlie asked where they met. Here, he said. We asked if he had children. He said he had a daughter of five and a boy of 20 days. We congratulated him. He said his wife was from Osaka. He had been in Japan but didn't like it, especially the raw fish, he said. We asked how his wife had adapted to Morocco. He said she was fine. "She can cook Moroccan food, cous-cous, tagine, anything", he said. We got to bed early having arranged to spend tomorrow night in the desert.

The room was initially stifling hot but we brought down the temperature with the air conditioning unit. Then Scharlie noticed a fresh breeze and cool air flow through the bathroom window causing eddies in the corridor. She opened the bedroom shutter and propped it with a couple of cautions. The bed was comfortable and the pillow soft. She turned off the light and practiced the route from bed to bathroom in the dark, first stubbing her toe on a packing case which formed the base of the extra bed, but avoided other hazards and had no problem in the night.

Friday 7 April Erg Chebbi

We had a lazy start. We didn't need to rush as our excursion to the desert for the night did not leave till 5pm at the earliest. Scharlie lay in bed, missing her morning cup of tea but enjoying the light filtering through the pale blue Berber window drape. Though a little quirky and DIY, the colours in this mud built house, the tiling, the cane ceiling, the plastered walls are all pleasing and satisfy one's need for beauty. The shower works well and we dressed and walked down the sandy Lane to the main hotel for breakfast. Hamid welcomes us. Breakfast is omelette, bread, orange juice, café au lait, strawberry jam, marmalade or honey and little cakes. It's hard not to eat too much.

Fran suggested we keep one of the houses to have as a base, Scharlie and I moved our stuff over and went for breakfast – nice coffee. Malachi and I played Suduko on my iPad.

Hamid suggested that we should walk in the dunes before it got too hot. So we set off in the car and drove to the base of the dunes where the camel caravans waited to take people into the desert.

We had thought the dunes would be just round the corner towards the date palms where the children were playing and that we could easily walk. But Hamid made his young brother show us the way in the car.

  The boy squeezes into the front seat with Malachi and we drive through the village towards the desert, down the dusty road bordered by flat roofed mud-built houses, reminding us of spaghetti westerns, and round the corner to our first glimpse of the desert.

  Postcard camels grouped against the date palms on the undulating sand but these are real. Four or five unfettered gambolling camels approach from our right swaying and ambling along then they quicken the pace until they are running with outstretched neck's streamlined and lower jaw and lips juddering. It is an extraordinary and funny sight.

We park the car near the grove of date palms. And head into the dunes. At first it's flat and hard underfoot and the sand is blackish but it soon becomes loose and shifting. Directly ahead of us in the distance is the highest dune rearing into the sky. On the top there are fleeting specks of people. It is a challenge. Keep to the ridge, says Fran, who is in the lead. It's a bit like walking in powder snow, but it doesn't stick to your feet. The thing is to contour and keep as level as possible. Where we misjudge the slope and had to go straight up to reach the ridge we have to climb on all fours.

It was quite tough climbing the dunes and Scharlie and I had to use our hands dig our toes in on the steep sections as if we were ice climbing. But it was worth it. There was a welcome strong cool breeze on our faces which neutralised the heat of the sun and we were very pleased to find ourselves on top more or less together.

Malachi tackled the sand mountain with his usual energy, bouncing and singing to himself and wanting to go first. He is barefooted and loves experimenting with the feel of the sand as he kicks it around. This sand is so pure and dry that it doesn't stick to your skin or leave a stain on your clothes. It's a warm orange colour and we find shirt pockets full at night but we shake it out without leaving a mark. You feel the curved shape the sand makes as you walk and the way the sensation changes with depth and how the temperature alters with the sun. Malachi was so full of energy that he even took on an extra steep slope on his way to the top and had to use his hands as well as his feet. Halfway up he became aware of the challenge he had set himself and we thought he'd slide down again but he paused, looked around, and kept going.

We sat on the knife-sculpted edge of the ridge in security and comfort. It moulds to your body like a beanbag and gives no sense of vertigo. Hamid had warned us of heart attacks from overexertion and we were a little concerned for a heavy breathing man who hauled himself up the last few metres with his daughter's help.

We could see the Tafilalt stretching away to the north, the line of wells leading from the tamarind tree at the base of the dunes towards the village. Turning round to the south there were more dunes stretching into Algeria, and then stony desert. We could see black tent camps, one of which where we will spend the night, and lines of camels moving sedately. We sat for a while, then surfed down and went back to the auberge to write.

A rest and late lunch of mixed salad and packing for our evening ride into

the desert Scharlie looked in the shop attached to the hotel. It was nice to be able to look at goods without being hassled. She bought a Berber tunic, an embroidered green Gandabi.

We had moved all our stuff into Fran's room and were ready by 5pm but our departure was delayed. We sat reading and writing all afternoon. till 5:30 when Hamid said his brother would take us over to the where the camels waited.

While waiting, Hamid's brother served us mint tea and then wound a long Berber deep blue coloured scarf around Malachi's head in Tuareg fashion, leaving one end free to be tucked across his mouth against wind or sand. Scharlie thought this would work much better on a camel than her cap, which might blow off in the wind. She chose a white one and Fran picked one in a silver-grey and had them expertly wound round their heads. Then we walked to meet our camels and our tall white-clad camel guide

Our camel driver is an old man with a nice smile we could see coming in the distance with his line of five camels. He had them kneel and then assign one to each of us. He had Steve climb on the dark brown lead camp. There were grey blankets with a metal saddle but it was still painful. You have to hold on tight as he had the camel stand or you would be thrown off. Nearly everyone we meet speaks English and our guide was no exception. Friendly and intelligent

with an empathetic sense of humour, he eyes us up and chooses a camel to suit. Scharlie was put on the smallest at the back and she swings her leg over the carpeted seat with surprising ease. The camels were made to kneel and their long legs folded like collapsible tables. Fran called out, hang on tight Scharlie, which stirred in her a dim memory of camel riding in Tunisia and she grabbed the pommel as the camel straightened its back legs tilting her violently forward, then upright, as its front legs followed.

Fran was next, then Mark, Malachi and Steve in the front. Our guide walked ahead holding a rope which linked all the camels. They were calm and cooperative animals and set off with a swaying motion. It was relaxing if you went with a swing and wasn't too tiring. Clearly the camels were very familiar with the route, which meandered in a south-easterly direction keeping to the crest of the lower dunes which undulated but steadily rose in altitude. Going uphill is comfortable but downhill stretches and puts great strain on your forearms, and you have to brace against the pommel to prevent yourself sliding over the neck of the camel. At one point Malachi's blanket slipped and he started sliding sideways, but with great agility righted himself.

We tramped for three quarters of an hour across the dunes. It was very beautiful and although we weren't really far away from civilisation one could

get a sense of the isolation of the desert. With evening light the colour of the sand changed from light to deep orange and the sky was violet blue. The wind rippled surface of the dunes into ever-changing patterns with the mesmerising effects of ripples on water. Occasional patches of blue-green feather leaved grasses catch the light and toss it about in the breeze. It is astonishingly beautiful.

About 40 minutes into the desert we stop on a higher dune and dismount and our guide leads us up the final sliding crest and we find ourselves looking down into a bowl at our encampment, a square of grey blanketed tents around a central space. A separate smaller shelter is the cookhouse. Inside the square there are three bedrooms. The whole structure is made from wooden

poles covered by blankets with extra support from canes, which grow in every oasis and are used a lot in local building. A large carpet covers the sand in the courtyard and in the dining space, low bench seating skirts the walls. In the bedrooms the sand is covered by the bed mattress, cushions and carpets.

There were other people here are already – Dutch as it turned out and two Korean girls. We dump our bags and went walking over the dunes. Malachi goes surfing sitting on a snowboard. Later the Tuareg boys took one of the boards out and went to play. I notice they didn't put their feet in the bindings, which seemed sensible. So I call Malachi over to see. He had no problems surfing down the sand in great style and was chuffed with himself. Scharlie and Steve climbed higher to get a brief glimpse of the sunset through the clouds.

We settled down in the dining tent and are served salad and chicken tagine. It was convivial by candlelight and Fran chatted about memories of childhood in Venezuela. Malachi went off read.

After dinner entertainment was drumming and singing. Two lads take turns to lead the drumming, powerfully coordinating intricate rhythms. Afterwards they taught Scharlie some rhythms and they played together. It was fun.

We'd been promised stars in the desert. But it was nearly full moon so not much chance of that, but Orion was clear. In bed the carpets flapped in the fresh breeze but the noise wasn't disturbing and we slept well. Scharlie had been concerned about the fact that there was no toilet facilities. Hamid said there is no one around, you just go behind the dunes. In fact with the number of dune buggies around it was hard to find a spot. Going out in the middle of the night was much easier and the stars bright when the moon had sunk to the horizon.

Saturday 8 April

We had an early start in the morning with no breakfast. The bed was hard and the pillow harder but we slept well and Steve woke just before six, dressed and went out to watch the sunrise. The sand was cold on the feet but the pink light on the dunes was very beautiful.

He climbed up and took photographs of two camels wandering about. Maybe they are left unattended and unbridled all night. Sometime before eight we set off back. Our driver hitched the camels together and Steve climbed aboard his big brown. But he must have been daydreaming because it reared up before he wasn't ready and he wasn't holding on. Despite this he kept his balance and stayed on. But it was a surprise from him, and an even bigger shock for the driver who used his hand to indicate his racing heart.

The shadows were still long on the dunes and the light soft. We were going down which is more difficult and it strains your arms leaning forward. Our driver talks to himself as he walks. He is wearing shoes today. It sounds as though he's having a conversation. He makes jokes and his hands move to emphasise his argument. Maybe the camels appreciate it. We are all finding it more painful than yesterday, except Malachi. We get back and breakfast and shower and get ready to leave.

Mountain

It's a long drive. Morocco is in a state of flux. Ancient mud houses and half finished apartment blocks. We go through a town, like the ones on the way north out of Fez with lots of new buildings and at least 20 banks. The road out of town is lined with elaborate street lamps seemingly leading nowhere.

Verdant groves of palms, almonds and figs are a welcome rest from the eyes. Then we see more rows of street lamps marking out what might become suburban streets. It was hard to imagine how all this building is being financed. It seems that there is a big push to develop the south, maybe for political reasons. But what the economy is based on is hard to guess. We wonder what sort of people will occupy these houses, if they are ever built, and where the water will come from to service them all. Have olives been displaced by real estate? Is all this development a waste, a misplaced optimism in the future of the country?

We stop to take a photograph of a Berber tent and realise that the molehills are mines. We climb one and looked down into mud tunnel so deep and narrow we can't see the bottom. Hard to believe people go down there digging. Fran says this is fossil country. There is a rickety windlass the miners used to lower themselves with and haul up the waste. It looks dangerous.

Malachi cottons on to a game, Ticking off the milestones which give the distance we have to go. He's a very good traveller for a 11-year-old and gets completely absorbed in any new thing he's trying. But eventually the driving palls and boredom sets in he declares like a child that he'd much rather have stayed at home. We've done everything now, he says. We've ridden the camels and been to three swimming pools and done our shopping!

We see snow on the high mountains and figure we are looking at Toubkal 4500m. We stop off for a coffee in Tinehir. The loo is squat style but clean as have all the ones we have encountered in restaurants or petrol stations. We stop for gas and vegetables for lunch and buy supplies from a supermarket. Supermarché stops are one Malachi's favourite refrains, which he sets to music, but we fail to find anywhere to stop for a picnic, so we keep going.

Scharlie takes a close-up photo of a date palm, which is young but fruiting heavily. I wonder how they harvest the fruit in such tall trees. They cut off all the old palm strands as they grow, but it would make for rough climbing.

Our next hotel, Chez Pierre, is in the Dades Gorge a detour from Boumaine. We reach the main turning to the gorge. We see ancient mud castles guarding this pass north through the High Atlas. Fran is anxious that the place should be nice after the last two nights. It's the most expensive she's booked so she has high expectations. But she's worried that it might not be what she is expecting.

Steve says, "remember how disappointed you were when we arrived in their goods but how much we liked it later".

We have only the name of the hotel and the gorge is many miles long. The sides are formed from what looks like crumbly red earth but on closer inspection it is more like concrete with an aggregate of huge boulders and small pebbles. Homes are built on the side of the road by scooping a house size space out of the side of the mountain. Where it is flat on the other side of the road there is a pleasant grove of dates and almonds, olives under-planted with barley wheat and some type of legume which the animals eat. Scarlet poppies brilliant in the sun find a home here too.

We passed by strange sandstone formations like Inca ruins. Fran would have like to stay here, but when we stop to ask at a patisserie the shopkeeper tells us we still have 7km to go. The gorge narrows and the views are not as interesting. Malachi has been patient all day but now it's wearing thin. I offer a prize of 20dh for the first to see our hotel. Malachi leans forward to block my view. We keep our eyes peeled and suspense is high as each corner brings a new view, some exciting, some dusty and boring. We are disheartened and Fran is feeling the full weight of responsibility from having done the booking. I think we're passed the best, she says.

Then suddenly round another dusty corner a hotel rears above us on the

right, sculpted out of the red cliff and set in terrace gardens as high as we can see. Malachi claims his prize. We arrive.

We park and climb the stairs to reception and the hotel staff help with our baggage. It is very grand. Our hotel is like a huge Victorian edifice clinging to the wall of the gorge. It reminds us of hotels in the South of France or the Italian Riviera. We are served mint tea and sweet peanut biscuits on the terrace under an almond tree – jasmine and roses and oleander are just beginning to bloom. It turns out that the huge hotel is empty and unused and

our apartments are single-storey buildings in the traditional Moroccan style set amongst the terrace garden, meandering paths and steps bordered by hedges of rosemary. It takes a little time to get used to and be sure you're on the right level.

It's been renovated recently. It's quite luxurious. Inside it is spacious and cool with tiled floors, a large sitting and dining area but no kitchen. The bathroom complex has toilet and modern white basin but only has cold water. A lobby leads to a curtained bath with shower over. And finally an alcove with a small round gleaming gold sink with hot and cold taps but a plug that doesn't fit. A hair dryer is plugged into the wall where it is sure to catch the spray from the tap, and the electric light switches are hard to find. The fake antique chests in our bedrooms have recently been stained and are giving off noxious fumes so Marc and Steve carry them out. It's a strange mixture of opulence and impracticality and, overall, is pleasant and welcoming.

We have our own terrace and deckchairs and in view of the gorge opposite. We sit and catch up on our journals.

A winding cleft in the mounting side looks like a watercourse and later the hotel manager, who had welcomed us and spoke English, says that when it rains there is a waterfall and torrent. It's as if the hotel has commissioned a spectacular water feature. To the left of the watercourse is an elegant beehive-shaped mud brick building and with binoculars we can see a man brushing the terrace outside. Above him and to the side there are neat terraces planted with fruit trees and vegetable. The manager tells us that a nomad family lives there. They will cultivate the land which the man has carved from the cliff from October to May then go into the high pasture with their goats in the summer. There are wadis and grazing there.

Scharlie wanders round the hotel terraces and sees that they are still building above the swimming pool. She talks to a man carrying a heavy bag on his back up the endless steps and asks him about it. He replies in English that it is 25 kg of sand. She say what a good job he is doing. He replies "thank you very much".

We watch a woman on the stony hillside opposite. She has a large sack on her back and is collecting herbs. She is selective and only takes certain plants. She's quartering the hillside systematically. A man appears with yellow sac and also starts collecting. They must live up here in huts on the hill and take their produce to market. The manager tells us that they are collecting thyme to sell in the village. He touches his fingers to his nose to show how well it smells. This is confirmed next morning when Mark relates how a group of five women appeared on the ridge with sacks and progress to the village stopping every so often to let the sun catch up with them.

It starts to get dark and at eight we descend to the restaurant. We're the first. Little groups have been waiting. Maybe they've been told they have to wait until eight. Anyway the place immediately fills up. We learn it's a set menu. Scharlie had asked about the menu earlier but the manager had said it's a surprise. "Are you vegetarian? I promise you no cous-cous or tagine", he said. "Our chef is renowned in this area and will make you a perfect dish". Scharlie was glad about this she had found the veg to be very overcooked and similar tasting whatever combination she'd tried.

Marc asks if the cuisine is French. The waiter says his brother is the chef and that the menu is a mixture of French Moroccan and other influences. Marc asked if they cooked with butter. He explains he has a severe allergy. to dairy He can't trust the cooking so he went back to our suite.

There were a number of courses – fried artichoke with avocado sauce, salad, cauliflower soup, stuffed chicken, a nice quiche and finally a panna cota desert.

We were finishing our main course when the lights went out and there was a sudden noise and about eight men filed in banging drums. They were carrying a cake and we realised that on the next table it was a young girl's birthday. We ordered desert. Malachi couldn't decide between chocolate or sorbet. He chose sorbet and luckily the girl brought him a piece of chocolate cake.

Sunday 9 April Dades Gorge to Finnt
We go to breakfast late. After we are sitting on one of the many terraces writing. Malachi goes swimming. Fran consults the guide and map and thinks about what we'd like to see. We have to pay in Sterling because we've run out of Dirham and they won't take cards.

We drive up the gorge. It narrows with high red sandstone walls either side and a big drop down to the river. We stop to take photographs. There are a couple of people deep in the gorge next to the river. I wonder how they managed to get down.

The edges of the road drop vertically and the flimsy stone barriers are missing in several places. We drive on to where the gorge begins to level out and there is a parking place and somewhere to turn. Marc and Steve watch a heavily laden lorry crawling up the switchbacks. The driver has to honk to

clear a tourist's car from a layby, because he has to do a three-point turn to get round the corners. Steve look's at the rock face speculatively looking for climbing lines. Scharlie and Fran barter for jewellery from a boy with a blanket shop next to the parking.

We drive back hoping to find an oasis for lunch and stop twice to take photographs of ancient Kasbah, castles guarding the pass. Malachi wants to climb on the pink monkeys fingers, the contorted rocks we've seen on the way up yesterday. So we find a place that looks like we can get down. We reach a sandy beach and clean swiftly flowing blue green water. Fran goes for a swim in the strong current and Malachi paddles. She has to walk back up as the flow is too strong. It is tranquil and green with giant poplar trees and date palms and groves of cane. There is only the sound of birds, a flock of black goats and a goatherd who smiles and says *Ca va*? Scharlie is glad she came down but is finding the scrambling difficult – her left knee won't bend or support her properly and her arms and wrists are aching. Malachi sweetly goes in front down the difficult bits and extends his arm to help. Scharlie says, I remember how as a child I was always the one that led the way!

After rejoining the main road the countryside is flat barren and featureless again with the bare mountains in the distance and more of these strange areas

marked by street lamps. We have been planning to stop at an oasis for lunch but Steve was confused by the roadsigns and we miss it. We reach Ouazazate and find our turn off. We drive through another of the incipient housing estates with lighting, roads and services along a stony road. Fran and Marc are worried, unsure we are on the right route. But it corresponds to the map so we press on for about 45 minutes on the bumpy road, going slowly because of the ridges. It must be a main route, we reason, because a number of four-wheel-drive vehicles pass us creating clouds of dust.

Scharlie had been feeling queasy and headachy for a while and the forty minutes of jolting and dust didn't help. It was hard to believe that anyone would make this journey but finally a steep curve led down to a parking lot at the edge of the river and a green oasis stretched away below us. A man was stationed there to ask if we were sleeping at the hotel. The track continued to bump and wind for another mile to a second man stationed to tell us we would soon be there, no problem. A final steep and rutted section caused Marc to stop the car and walk round the corner and inspect the hill before attempting, it in spite of the vigourous assurances of our outpost. But then we were there and looking up at a smart modern white painted building and porters anxious to carry our luggage. Four or five other cars were parked.

Climbing to the terrace we had a panoramic view of the oasis and surrounding sandstone hills, villages and mountains beyond.

There was a fracas on arrival when we had to produce our passports fill in forms. Scharlie couldn't find hers where she was sure she put it on the inside pocket of her suitcase. We were faced with the prospect of messing up the holiday for everyone by spending the last day in the British Consulate. She unpacked everything and checked each item down to the last sock. It wasn't there and she had no explanation for its loss. Are you sure I didn't give it to you and you have it somewhere, she said hesitantly to Steve. I gave it to you to look after yourself, he said, looking white and anxious.

Fran recounted her experiences of losing her passport and how she now always carried it with her in a body bag. We were being forced to conclude it had been stolen from the suitcase. Malachi took it all in and Steve sat with his head in his hands thinking. Then quietly he stood up and walked over to his black backpack and drew my passport out of pocket. Malachi whooped. "Grandee's got it. Grandee's got it! It's hilarious!" Steve and I were too shaken and relieved to say anything and just hugged each other. Fran said it's not at all hilarious it's a huge relief. After that Scharlie was able to lie down for an hour or so and nurse her headache. It eased a little as the temperature cooled.

Fran changed her room to get one with a window onto the courtyard. The sun loungers round the pool were occupied but she and Malachi wasted no time in plunging in. The bedrooms and bathrooms are large and the beds have soft pillows.

Dinner, in the large dining room, was the usual tagine – this time with almonds. We shared couscous – Steve ate the chicken and Scharlie had the veg. The stars were out, but there is a full moon. The frogs are melodious quite different from tropical frogs in Venezuela and Jamaica. We sleep well but Scharlie is feeling ill, either from the heat today or something she ate.

Monday 10 April Finnt to Aït Benhaddou
By the time we get to breakfast nearly everyone has left. Steve went for a walk by the side of the canal along the river. There are small plots or allotments with vines for raisins, grain and greens. He walks a mile or so. Women are cutting plants and another woman is leading a donkey with a load of green stuff.

Fran and Malachi enjoyed the swimming pool last night and we stayed on this morning so they could have more time in the pool. Scharlie also felt a little better for the rest. We had been booked to stay here two nights but were so put off by the bumpy ride that Fran cancelled and booked for a hotel in Aït Benhaddou, enroute to Marrakesh. It wasn't far away so we had time to stop in the oasis.

We set off but soon after we start Fran suggests that we walk by the river. Scharlie and Steve get out and go on paddle and Marc dropped us off and we find our way through the groves, over palms and fruit trees, broad beans and barley to the sandy plain through which the river meanders. The river is warm and Steve goes back to persuade Malachi to come down. He enjoys himself chasing frogs and throwing stones.

The water has cut multiple channels through the sound and everywhere we look there are small frogs, some green, some brown. Males apparently green from the positions adopted by one mating pair. It was cool and refreshing paddling up the river to where Marc waited. With the frogs croaking and the birds singing it was pleasant and hard to leave.

We wade along the river. It's most pleasant in the warm water walking on the soft sand. We walk as far as the ford and Marc drives down to pick us up. It was worth walking. We've decided we like this place. It's becoming a pattern

– we are suspicious when we arrive and don't like it, but then we do, a lot! How English.

It wasn't far so we decided to stop in Ouazazate to look for carpets. We retrace our steps to the city with its imposing main street. It's hot and bright and Scharlie still felt unwell. While looking for a parking place to park we spot another cooperative carpet shop with a carpet hanging on the wall outside of a similar design to the one we loved in Fes.

The proprietor had a gentle low-key approach. He explained how that type of carpet was made and called it a "marriage carpet". He explained that many women were in the Co-op. The Berber women made the carpets as a wedding dowry and gave them to the groom's family. In return the women received gold jewellery, much of it threaded gold coins. Most of the carpets were made by widows or divorcees.

We asked the price of the large carpet we liked. He brought it in and spread it on the floor, together with a blue one that Fran liked. They are of similar design, but different colours. Scharlie said the one she'd chosen reminded her of the desert. The man gave us a price for the two. We said we'd go for a coffee and come back.

We walked into town along the main street and found a supermarket

and a cash exchange. Then we went for coffee and Malachi had pizza. Fran went shopping round the corner and bought a jewelled clothes pin she liked, Malachi bought a Tuareg dagger and Scharlie bought a necklace. Fran and Steve calculated how much we were prepared to pay and how much we should offer. He had said 8200dh, about £650. We decided to offer 4000. Fran went on her own and bargained. She came out and said he gone down to 6000dh, still more than we'd agreed. So Steve went in with her and offered 5000. The bargaining went back and forth. He said you bargain like a Berber, which was flattering. We settled on 5500 a discount of 33%, which was exactly what we set as our price. So everyone was happy.

Marc really liked our carpet and agreed it was reminiscent of the desert. The man rolled them tightly and wrapped them in black plastic. We paid. He counted the money carefully and gave us a receipt. We shook hands all smiles.

We drove out of town and it didn't take as long to reach our next stop, Aït Benhaddou. We stopped to take photographs of the Kasbah and decided to come back and climb up to it when it was cooler. The hotel was easy to find in the central town there was a pool and Malachi went swimming. Although the rooms were cramped it was fine for one night.

Rather than climb the Kasbah with all the tourists we drive up the valley 9 km

to Tamdaght. We'd read that it was more authentic and there was an ancient Glaoui Kasbah. We park near camels in front of a ruined castle and go to explore. A man arrives just after I've entered the courtyard. He offers to show us around, which was just as well since we aren't sure what is safe to walk on.

The Kasbah dates back to the seventh century. The red mud walls are crumbling, eroded by rain, but the lower rooms still have the original tiles,

doors, balconies. There's a wall with a placard listing at least 25 films that have been made here. He showed us the salon of the pasha with its decorative balcony where they filmed the scene in Gladiator when Oliver Reed instructs Maximus in "the art of pleasing the crowd". It's very atmospheric. We go up on the roof and see a stork on its nest on the tower. We learn that they filmed scenes in Prince of Persia and Alexander here.

Our guide offers to take us to the garden we can see below. It's tricky traversing round the base of the castle. We have a precipitous climb and step round a corner on a narrow ledge below the outside wall. There is maybe 4-5 acres of land with a mix of produce, irrigated by a clay conduit. It's all very beautiful and ordered in a delightfully relaxed way. Almond trees and roses grow above peas and beans and wheat and lots of other edible plants and herbs. It's criss-crossed in a chequerboard of paths bounded by hedges of wild roses. In the markets they sell dried sweet smelling rosebuds – perhaps they are grown for this purpose. Scharlie spots clumps of species gladioli flowering in the grain, similar to *gladiolus byzantium*, but paler pink.

On the way back to the car the guide takes us to a show like an Aladdin's cave, with beautiful jewellery. Coral beads cost 100dh per gram. We smile and say *au revoir*. There are two luxurious hotels. We have a glimpse of a beautiful courtyard that looks exclusive and expensive. An elegant woman walks past with a porter pushing a cart piled high with expensive luggage. We go back to our hotel to probably the least distinguished meal of the holiday and an early night.

Tuesday 11 April Aït Benhaddou to Marrakesh

We rise early, breakfast and get away in good time. The road over the mountains, the Tizi n'Tichka pass (2260m) is exciting with its endless switchbacks. It is dry on the south side of the mountains and teams of men are repairing the road. The rock is unstable and it looks like a continual job to keep the road clear of rocks and slides. They are putting huge effort into improving this route, which is used by trucks and tourists alike. It seems to be under continual repair. The method is to scrape the stony hillside on the inside of a bend and dump out on the outside thus gradually creating a wider space. This earth and rock is rolled until this is firm enough and tarmac finishes the job. Surveyor with post and theodolite are a frequent sight. When we are forced to the outside edge of a road by an oncoming lorry you don't feel very comfortable.

We stop in a layby and are accosted by an old man selling geodes. Most of the ones we've been offered along the road are garishly painted in pink or multicolour. This man had a nice clear white crystal geode and Fran buys it.

It got much greener on the north side of the coll and the opposite slope was terraced with fruit trees and small plots of wheat. We had bought bread in the village and look for a place to picnic.

We find a layby where we can scramble down rocks to the river and have lunch. Remarkably we aren't hassled to buy anything. More and more wild flowers are appearing and here there are clumps of French lavender. Scharlie reaches for her iPhone camera, and to her horror is not in her pants pocket. She says she knows exactly which route she'd taken and Steve walks back with her and finds it is lying on an open sandy stretch below the bolder she had climbed over.

Marrakesh

We get to Marrakesh easier than we expected. Fran is excited and keen to get her bearings and work out where we will be staying. She wants to find the main mosque which she used to use as a starting point. But we've come in on the other side of the city and it's impossible to find anywhere to park. We stop so I can get the guide out of the boot to help Frances navigate.

A man on a motorbike says hello and asks me where we trying to get to. I tell him. He offers to show us. But Fran wants to try and do it herself and Marc is put out by being hassled constantly by boys asking for money, hawkers and would-be guides. We try to get away but seem to be stuck with him and he leads us to the car park near the main mosque that Fran knows.

We get there and park but Fran is upset. The man wants to help get us to our hotel, Fran wants to walk. She says it is through the Souk. I leave them arguing. I'm worried though about finding our way dragging our suitcases through crowds of tourists. We decide we'll go for a coffee and allow Fran

to get her bearings. While I'm waiting the man tells me we can drive and that there is safe parking right near the hotel. I suggest we use him Fran reluctantly agrees.

It's only a short walk from the parking court to the Riad, the garden house were we are staying. It's a lovely quiet house with a series of rooms on two floors around a central courtyard. We get two rooms on the first floor. We have a short rest and Fran, Malachi and Steve set off to explore the city. Scharlie was still feeling unwell and extremely glad to open the windows and draw the curtains against sun and lie down.

We want to get acclimatised to the area and be able to find our way around. We turn right at the end of our alley and follow our noses along the maze of passages to a main street of shops. From there we walk to the main square and find a cafe for coffee and ice cream. There are snake charmers in the square banging a drum and playing pipes. Street sellers are setting up their stalls and lighting fires to start cooking.

We wander on and find the courtyard of antiques where Bashir worked that Fran knew from her previous visits. From there we went in search of Muhammad. He was the man Francis had told us about and with whom she had done most business. She said he was an artisan who could make anything

and, 10 years ago, henna lamps were one of his specialties. But despite walking a long way we failed to find it. We did, however, get taken round the smelly tannery. We also have various run-ins with supposed guides wanting to take us to their uncle's shops.

Fran came back confident and happy to have found her mosque and square and got her internal map and sense of direction functioning again.

We went back to the square in the evening to a rooftop pizzeria to please Malachi. We're tired of soggy vegetable tagine and Scharlie has basil pesto pasta. The square below is jammed with jostling people and we can hear frenzied piping and drums. Steve says it's snake charmers with a cobra. Scharlie doesn't look because she remembers seeing one in India.

Wednesday 12th April
We tried to get away early. We plan to go to a garden, the *Jardin Majorelle*. It was the inspiration for a recent Chelsea winner. But we lingered over breakfast and didn't get there to 9:30. The garden was created by Jacques Majorelle, an artist, in the 30s from a date palmerie on the edge of the city. Fran loves this place and spent many hours here, coming in the early morning or evening. She didn't want to get caught by crowds of tourists and it seemed she might give

it a miss. There were a number of parties before us, but once we entered the garden they seemed to disappear and it didn't seem crowded.

It was cool and tranquil and very beautiful. The majesty of the arching bamboo avenue imposed its calm and it possible to take photographs that were not plastered with other tourists. The garden has a formal grid pattern of pools, arbours and gazebos which you become aware of as you explore. Marc says it's a Zen-like experience. Unlike formal European gardens there is no point at which you can see the overall layout – is intimate and sensual rather than imposing. The tall palms and bamboo link you to the spaciousness of the sky but give shade, so the riotous colours of a scarlet or purple bougainvillea

climbing 20 feet or so into the trees are caught by the shafts of sun to shine like silken raiment.

A long rill traverses the centre of the garden from a gazebo in the bamboo avenue to a fantastic pavilion of deep blue. The broad paths are polished scarlet and run trhough an amazing collection of cacti in shades of silver grey and fuzz of pale gold. One specimen about 3m high was covered in white fragrant flowers and the scent of its perfume filled the air. It was clear you should keep to the paths as the cacti, young palms and exotic trees were planted in raked sand. The only intruder to leave its footprints was a black and white cat playing with a drooping palm leaf.

After Majorelle's death in 1978 his house and garden deteriorated and the site was due for demolition when it was bought by Yves St Laurent who rescued it. At his death it was taken over by a French foundation and the house turned into a Berber Museum. Walking round the museum we were struck by how similar Berbers' lifestyle was to Jews in the old Testament and also by how small they were.

We were there about three hours. Most of the tourist groups were there only 10 or 20 minutes. Fran had never been in the Berber museum before. It was as interesting as the garden. Fran was enthralled by the jewellery, artefacts and costumes. There was video showing the building of a Kasbah using rammed earth walls, splitting palm logs for the floor beams and using cane to support the clay roof.

On the way back we pass a supermarket and buy provisions. On the road just outside the Medina's walls we find a bank and change money and then see a photographic studio displaying black and white photos of old Marrakesh. Steve wanted to go in and persuaded the others to stop. Fran and Steve sift through dozens of photos and choose some to buy.

We got home and while the others rested Fran and Steve went out in search of Mohammad. We took the main drag into the Souk. We made our way through the leather workers and people making shoes and belts. Fran said she didn't recognise anything, it was all different. The whole area has been cleaned up and renovated. Suddenly, almost after we've given up, we came to a small square and she stopped, looked around and said it's here. An old man recognised her and said Mohammed would be back in 10 minutes. There is a

cafe and we order coffee and sit and wait.

We were chatting when a small handsome man arrived, his face beaming with smiles. Fran and he hugged. Fran introduced me. We chatted and he took us into his shop and showed us round. He's no longer making henna lamps and has gone retail. We admired his handiwork.

He took us upstairs and pulled out seats for us and sat on a low stool in

front of a crude hand lathe. He cut a piece of wood help from a round stick and fixed it between the two centres made from cast iron nails. He lubricated the ends of the wood with some clear liquid from a bottle that he applied with a long steel needle. He released one end of the piece and wound the string of a bow round it. He then worked the string with water to keep it cool. He gave it a tentative couple of turns to make sure it was centred and hit the piece of

wood with a handle of his chisel to adjust it. He was very deft and quick. Using a single chisel he fashioned a wooden pendant about 3 inches long. Before he severed it from the stock he drilled a hole with his bow and a string. The really interesting thing was how he used his right foot and big toe almost like an extra hand to direct the chisel's angled cutting edge since his own right hand was occupied pushing the bow. We said goodbye, Fran promising to come back later with Malachi and Marc.

We found the metalworkers and a couple of trays that might do for Scharlie. We took photos to show her later. The man initially asked 900dh but as we walked off, he held Steve's arm and whispered for you 350dh before we could tear ourselves away, laughing. And Fran found a lamp she liked. It was a flat oval role rather than a globe and the design was very pretty. Again we said we'd come back.

Steve was planning on sunbathing and had gone to the roof terrace when Fran came and said she couldn't go back to see Mohammad carrying a lamp and a tray. So Steve said he'd come and carry them back.

We set off about five and found the metalworkers easily. We bargain. We are prepared to walk away. Fran didn't think we'd get anything because she was thrown when the lamp man said 1800dh for the lamp she liked as she'd

remembered him saying 800dh. Nevertheless she got the tray down to 250dh. And she managed to get the lamp for 500dh which was a little more than she'd wanted to pay but still okay.

We had run out of time because Mohammed said he'd wait to 6 and it was now after. Steve left them set off back on his own with the trailer lamp. He did alright at first, following the way he remembered, but somewhere he missed his way and went marching down a main thoroughfare when he should have turned into the Souk. He kept going east thinking he would join our street further north but reached the Medina wall. So he turned back and retraced his steps south to the main square. He was walking down a crowded street when he recognised holes in the canvas awning overhead and realised he was at the end of our alley. He had a shower and 10 minutes on the terrace in the sinking sunlight. Scharlie bought the silver tray Steve had spotted earlier

We went out to dinner. Scharlie stayed home. Fran has been very disappointed with the food here. She used to eat with families when she came 15 years ago and said that the vegetables were not overcooked and bland. The only meal Fran has really enjoyed was a lamb tagine she had with Steve in a restaurant she used to go to in the main square.

This Riad is tranquil and the interior decoration is simple and pleasing. The

shower is most innovative, crafted by local plasters. It's a restful place to be. When the day cooled Scharlie went up to the rooftop terrace to enjoy the view with the plants and cats. You really could walk from house to house across the roofs.

Steve had a delicious harari soup of spicy tomato and beans. Malachi and Steve played cheat while we waited for ice cream desert. Early bed.

Thursday 13 April
We had breakfast. The landlady asked about Steve's writing. We walked to the parking. It was fairly easy to find our way out of town. But the journey was the longest yet – nine hours. We didn't have a hotel booked and hoped to find somewhere on the way.

This route is much less touristy than the southern route and is much more agricultural. The first half was open plain with the distant mountains hidden in the list. Olive grows, cornfields ripening and sheep. A series of towns with half-finished houses and lots of new development.

We thought of going to the Cascades d'Ouzoud, a popular tourist day-out from Marrakesh, but decided against it. We stopped at Kasba-Tadla to have

a coffee and soon after turned off the road towards Imilchil on a road that the guidebook said had dangerous precipitous bends. We didn't go far and stopped before it started to climb and had lunch in an olive grove.

The second part of the journey was very pretty – heavy with flowers, patches of wheat and fruit trees in blossom. Blood-red fields of poppies, beautiful women in red and gold embroidered outfits with hoods riding donkeys. Difficult road under repair in places, bordered by an irrigation trough that ran for miles with branches into villages. Dangerous double overtakes on blind hills and unseen bends. People by the road asking for lifts. Crowds of children going to afternoon school. Later we saw other children leaving other schools, their mood quite different; fooling around happy to be out. A young man exercising a black Arab stallion. Herds of horses running free.

Ifrane

It became clear that there wouldn't be any hotels en route, so we looked at the guidebook and picked a hotel in Ifrane and rang and booked. We arrive soon after seven, dump the bags and go to eat.

Ifrane is an mock French Alpine village. The main hotel is called the Chamonix. It's all very clean and European. There is supposed to be skiing here in the winter. Maybe it was a hill station for the French administrators and army chiefs. It is now expanding dramatically with estates of expensive chalet homes for rich Moroccans. Scharlie and Steve have cauliflower soup. We got back to the hotel to find the central heating wanging away. We had just managed to turn it off when the receptionist came to fix it. He had thought we were too cold. Moroccans obviously feel the cold.

Friday 14 April

We had a lazy start and went to the patisserie in the village. It was good – croissant and café au lait. We tried to find a path we'd seen on the map in the hotel but failed and went back and asked the receptionist like Scharlie had wanted to do in the first place. He said that despite the photos of bubbling waterfalls, the rivers would be dry at this time of the year, but that there was a walk just round the corner. We set off and after a short stretch of road deviated right into the forest and started climbing. At first it was new conifer

planting on stony terraces that had destroyed the alpine flora. There are plenty of signs of beer parties around camp fires. But as we climbed higher vegetation change to ancient oak forest with peonies and Solomon's Seal and wild red pepper. We got to the top of the little mountain before turning back.

Back on the road we saw car stop to avoid running over something. The driver gets out and places whatever it is carefully on the stony embankment. We looked to see what it was. Marc lingered to look and had obviously found something, so we went back to see. It was a large venerable tortoise. Malachi held it and we carried it to where the fence ended and it could climb the hill.

We stopped to buy nuts and figs at the roadside stall. We've seen lots of police stationed along our route and wondered if the King and someone important was coming. But the nut seller said it was a bike race. The traffic was stopped so we waited. It meant we were late getting to the airport.

Fez

At the airport, we waited under the shade of a tree on the grass and made lunch of tuna while Marc sorted the car. We got back to our house in Fez. Mohammed met us above the square and helped us carry the carpets. It's nice to be back. We made tea. It feels like we've been away a long while. Fran went out and bought veg for dinner.

Saturday 15 April

Fran and Scharlie went out shopping while Malachi and Steve played chess and draughts. Fran and Scharlie returned with blankets, pottery and an amazing necklace. They also brought back cardboard boxes and parcel tape and we made two big parcels of our purchases and taped on big address labels.

   We got to bed early but the neighbourhood kids were noisy, playing in the alley just outside our bedroom window. The tone of their play was just like that of English children at play. Finally we got to sleep.

Sunday 16 April Fez to UK

The alarm woke us at four and we got up and dressed. We set off up the steep road to the Batha Square and arrived exactly at 5am. The taxi driver came and the journey back home to the UK was easy and uneventful.

www.ingramcontent.com/pod-product-compliance
Lightning Source LLC
Chambersburg PA
CBHW041616220426
43671CB00001B/12